NASCAR

AUTHORIZED HANDBOOK
All You Need to Know to Get Ready for the 2005 NASCAR NEXTEL Cup Series!
written by Jim Gigliotti and K.C. Kelley

CONTENTS

Reader's Digest
Children's Books

Pleasantville, New York • Montréal, Québec • Bath, United Kingdom

The Chase Is On!

What a finish! The first year of the Chase for the NASCAR NEXTEL Cup ended with a thrilling finish, as Kurt Busch held off Jimmie Johnson to win NASCAR's top prize. It was the closest finish in NASCAR history! The 2005 season looks to be another great ride!

In 2004, NASCAR used its special "playoff" for the first time to determine its champion. After the first 26 races, the top 10 drivers were given new point totals (see box); only by being in the top 10 could a driver win the season title.

Jeff Gordon started in the lead, but Dale Earnhardt Jr., Jimmie Johnson, and Kurt Busch all spent time in the leader's seat. Johnson started slowly, but won four of the final five races. Gordon won two races as well, and was in the hunt until the final laps of the final race. Kurt Busch proved that "sure and

Top Ten

The Chase Begins Driver/Points	The Chase Ends Driver/Points
1. Jeff Gordon/5,050	**1.** Kurt Busch/6,506
2. Jimmie Johnson/5,045	**2.** Jimmie Johnson/6,498
3. Dale Earnhardt Jr./5,040	**3.** Jeff Gordon/6,490
4. Tony Stewart/5,035	**4.** Mark Martin/6,399
5. Matt Kenseth/5,030	**5.** Dale Earnhardt Jr./6,368
6. Elliott Sadler/5,025	**6.** Tony Stewart/6,326
7. Kurt Busch/5,020	**7.** Ryan Newman/6,180
8. Mark Martin/5,015	**8.** Matt Kenseth/6,069
9. Jeremy Mayfield/5,010	**9.** Elliott Sadler/6,024
10. Ryan Newman/3,255	**10.** Jeremy Mayfield/6,000

steady" would win it all. He finished in the top six in each of the first six races, taking the lead in the fifth week of the Chase. He held on during a tense Ford 400 in Miami to win it all.

As the 2005 season began, everyone was back in the race, and aiming for one goal: Make it into the Chase for the NASCAR NEXTEL Cup—and then floor it for 10 races to take the title.

The Champion!

Kurt Busch enters the 2005 season as the defending NASCAR NEXTEL Cup champion! He's come a long way in a short time. Kurt started racing at the age of 14 on small tracks in his native Nevada, winning several championships in various types of cars. Team owner Jack Roush recognized Kurt's talents early and hustled him into the top series in 2000. Four years later, he was the champ. Kurt's brother, Kyle, will join him in NASCAR NEXTEL Cup racing in 2005.

Kurt Busch

Track Tour

NASCAR tracks range from enormous superspeedways to tight-turned shorter tracks and twisting road courses. If you have ever been to a track, you know just how enormous they are. Here are some features you'll find at nearly every track.

Grandstand: Fans sit all around the track in huge risers full of benches or individual seats.

Track: This ribbon of asphalt and concrete is the centerpiece of any track. Some tracks are wider than others, but all have to have enough room for the cars to battle for position.

Apron: The area of the track surface nearest the center of the track is called the apron. A yellow or white line shows drivers where they should go to stay on the track. However, they can drive on the apron to avoid trouble or if their car isn't working right.

Infield & Garages: In the center of the track itself is the enormous, flat infield area. This is the main area where most of the team transporters are parked. You'll also find the garage area where cars are prepared before races. Week after week, race teams set up huge garage areas from scratch. They bring tools, engines, parts, and other gear, ready to do whatever it takes to win.

Pit road: Along one side of most tracks is the long, road-like area where teams set up their pit-stop positions. Each team is assigned one spot where their driver can stop during races.

Press box: High above the track is where the TV crews sit, watching the race and describing it to millions of fans.

Starter's booth: Above the start-finish line is a small platform that sticks out over the track. From there, an official waves flags to tell drivers to start, stop, slow down, or that the race is over.

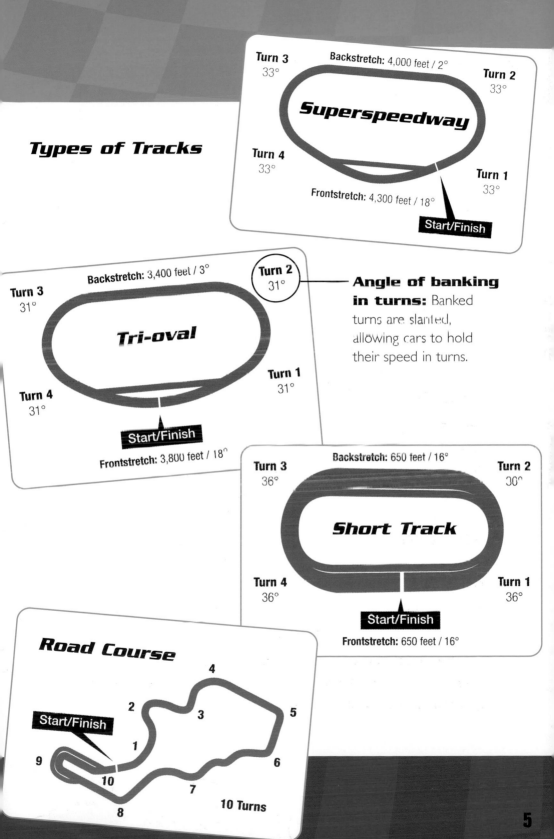

Types of Tracks

Superspeedway

Turn 3
33°

Backstretch: 4,000 feet / 2°

Turn 2
33°

Turn 4
33°

Turn 1
33°

Frontstretch: 4,300 feet / 18°

Start/Finish

Tri-oval

Backstretch: 3,400 feet / 3°

Turn 3
31°

Turn 2
31°

Turn 4
31°

Turn 1
31°

Start/Finish

Frontstretch: 3,800 feet / 18°

Angle of banking in turns: Banked turns are slanted, allowing cars to hold their speed in turns.

Short Track

Backstretch: 650 feet / 16°

Turn 3
36°

Turn 2
30°

Turn 4
36°

Turn 1
36°

Start/Finish

Frontstretch: 650 feet / 16°

Road Course

Start/Finish

1
2
3
4
5
6
7
8
9
10

10 Turns

What They Drive

You've probably heard the term "stock car" before. It's part of NASCAR's official name, the National Association for Stock Car Auto Racing. But what is a "stock" car? Stock refers to a standard design, to the stock or supply of cars a car dealer keeps on hand. In NASCAR's early days, drivers simply took their regular, or stock, cars out to the track to race. As technology improved, cars were designed just to race, but the tradition of modeling them after standard cars continues.

Today's cars are the products of months of planning, research, and design. Experts use computers to create the perfect shape for cutting through the wind. Under the metal skin is a skeleton of heavy steel tubing welded together to form a protective cage. Dozens and dozens of additional parts are used to create a safe car for drivers to race.

Parts of the Car

Some of the key parts of every NASCAR stock car include:

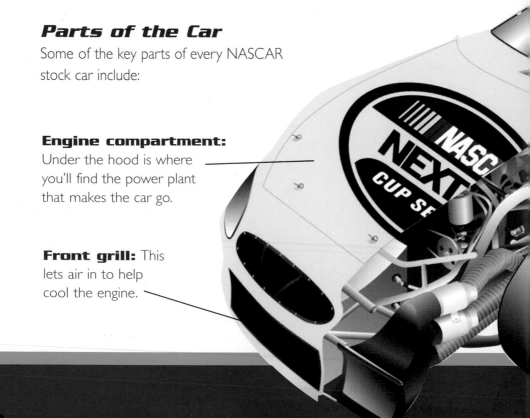

Engine compartment: Under the hood is where you'll find the power plant that makes the car go.

Front grill: This lets air in to help cool the engine.

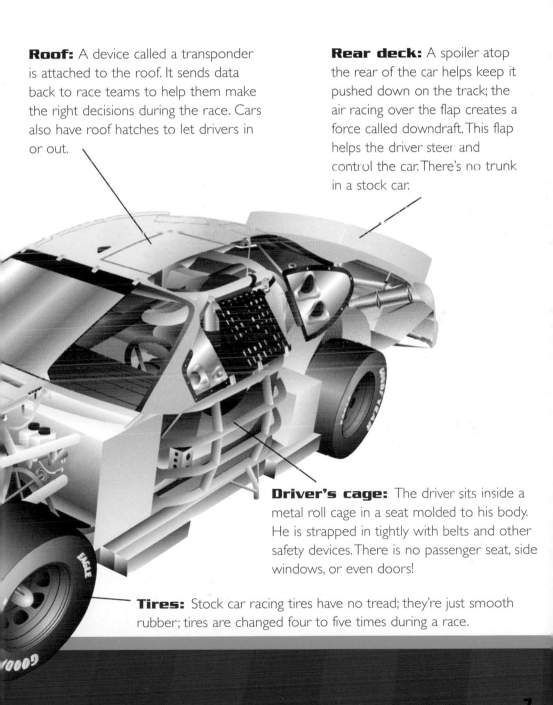

Roof: A device called a transponder is attached to the roof. It sends data back to race teams to help them make the right decisions during the race. Cars also have roof hatches to let drivers in or out.

Rear deck: A spoiler atop the rear of the car helps keep it pushed down on the track; the air racing over the flap creates a force called downdraft. This flap helps the driver steer and control the car. There's no trunk in a stock car.

Driver's cage: The driver sits inside a metal roll cage in a seat molded to his body. He is strapped in tightly with belts and other safety devices. There is no passenger seat, side windows, or even doors!

Tires: Stock car racing tires have no tread; they're just smooth rubber; tires are changed four to five times during a race.

Greg Biffle

Stats

Born: December 23, 1969

Birthplace: Vancouver, WA

NASCAR debut: 2002

Career victories: 3*

* as of the start of the 2005 season

In 2002, Greg Biffle was the season points champion in the series just below the NASCAR NEXTEL Cup. In 2003 and 2004, he proved he belonged in the top NASCAR series with consecutive top-20 finishes in the overall standings. (He was 20th in 2003 and tied for 17th in 2004). Now, in 2005, Greg is hoping to graduate to the next level—being a contender for the NASCAR NEXTEL Cup championship.

Most NASCAR observers think he's got plenty of potential and time to do that. Greg turned 35 in the off-season and still is a relative newcomer to the NASCAR NEXTEL Cup Series. However, he already has a couple of major championships under his belt. In addition to his series win in 2002, Greg won the NASCAR Craftsman Truck series in 1998. He is the only driver in history to win the title in those two NASCAR Series.

Although Greg did not seriously contend for the NASCAR NEXTEL Cup Series title in 2004, he still had a major impact on the final standings. When he held off Jimmie Johnson and Jeff Gordon down the stretch to win the Ford 400 in the year's final race, that allowed his Roush Racing teammate, Kurt Busch, to capture the season points title.

2004 Results

Races: 35
Points: 3,902
Overall finish: 17th (tie)
Victories: 2
Top-5 finishes: 4
Top-10 finishes: 8

FAST FACTS

♦ Greg closed the season strong in 2004. He had just one top-10 finish during the first half of the season, but added seven in the second half.

♦ All three of Greg's career victories (entering 2005) have come on superspeedways. His first was at Daytona in the 2003 Pepsi 400.

> **66** *This just goes to show everybody what the No. 16 car is capable of doing.* **99**

—Greg Biffle, after struggling much of the 2004 season, then coming on strong to win the final race of the season in Miami.

Jeff Burton

Stats

Born: June 29, 1967
Birthplace: South Boston, VA
NASCAR debut: 1993
Career victories: 17*

*as of the start of the 2005 season

After a year of transition, Jeff Burton enters the 2005 season with renewed hopes for a long-awaited points championship. Jeff began the 2004 season driving the No. 99 car for Roush Racing. In August, however, he switched to the Richard Childress Racing Team and car No. 31. This year, he'll be in the No. 30 car for the Childress team and will keep the same crew chief.

Jeff and his fans hope that the new team affiliation helps him fulfill the potential he showed in 1994 when he first broke into the NASCAR series full-time. He was the NASCAR Raybestos Rookie of the Year that season as he finished 24th in the standings. After that, he gradually improved to as high as third place in 2000, and a points championship seemed to be a real possibility.

Since then, however, Jeff's fortunes have gradually declined. He last won a race in 2001, and he ended up with a 18th-place finish in the points standings last year. The upside of his midseason switch to Childress, though, was a trial run with his new team, and he closed the season with three top-10 finishes down the stretch.

2004 Results

Races: 36
Points: 3,902
Overall finish: 18
Victories: 0
Top-5 finishes: 2
Top-10 finishes: 6

FAST FACTS

♦ Jeff finished among the top five in the points standings for four consecutive years beginning in 1997, capping the stretch with his third-place finish in 2000.

♦ Jeff got a full-time ride in the NASCAR series in 1994; his older brother, Ward, made his NASCAR Cup Series debut that same season.

❝ *I'm as upbeat about my career as I've been. There's a renewed energy and a renewed sense of urgency.* **❞**

—Jeff Burton, who moves into a new car with
Richard Childress Racing in 2005.

Kurt Busch

Stats

Born: August 4, 1978
Birthplace: Las Vegas, NV
NASCAR debut: 2000
Career victories: 11*

*as of the start of the 2005 season

At just 26 years old and in only his fourth full season, Kurt Busch won the first NASCAR NEXTEL Cup Series championship in 2004. He held off several challengers down the stretch to win the closest points chase in the history of NASCAR.

Though Kurt's rise to the top of the stock car racing world was rapid by almost any standard, it was not without its speed bumps. In fact, it appeared that Kurt would cruise to the championship when he won the Sylvania 300 to open the first Chase for the NASCAR NEXTEL Cup, then finished no worse than sixth in the next five races.

But he blew an engine and placed 42nd at the Bass Pro Shops MBNA 400 four races from the end and, suddenly, a slew of competitors were on his rear fender. Then, with five drivers still in the hunt for the title going into the season-ending Ford 400 in Homestead, Florida, Kurt suffered a broken wheel early in that race. He made a dramatic entrance into pit road on three wheels—just missing a separating wall—got his car fixed, and got back on track. His fifth-place finish in the race was barely enough to edge Jimmie Johnson for the overall title by eight points.

Now the question is, what does Kurt do for an encore in 2005?

2004 Results

Races: 36
Points: 6,506
Overall finish: 1st
Victories: 3
Top-5 finishes: 10
Top-10 finishes: 21

FAST FACTS

♦ Before Kurt's eight-point victory over Jimmie Johnson for the 2004 points championship, the closest finish in NASCAR history had been 10 points (Alan Kulwicki's margin over Bill Elliott in 1992).

♦ Kurt's younger brother, Kyle, was the Raybestos Rookie of the Year in the series just below the NASCAR NEXTEL Cup Series in 2004.

" *We beat the best of the best over ten races, and to have my name along the best names in history, it means so much to me.* **"**

—Kurt Busch, after holding off some of the biggest names in NASCAR to win his first points title in 2004.

Dale Earnhardt Jr.

Stats

Born: October 10, 1974
Birthplace: Kannapolis, NC
NASCAR debut: 1999
Career victories: 15*

*as of the start of the 2005 season

For a long time, Richard Petty represented the face of NASCAR. Then it was Dale Earnhardt Sr. (Dale Jr.'s father). Jeff Gordon was the most popular driver for a new generation of stock car fans in the 1990s. But today, it is Dale Earnhardt Jr.'s turn at the wheel. He is perhaps stock car racing's most dominant personality.

Unfortunately for Earnhardt's legions of fans, that distinction has not translated into a NASCAR points championship yet. He was one of the favorites to take home the coveted title last season and began the year with an emotional victory at the Daytona 500. One month later, he won again at the Golden Corral 500, and he appeared to be on his way to the crown.

Ultimately, it didn't happen. A midseason practice lap for a sports car race during a break in the NASCAR schedule resulted in a crash. A late-season penalty and back-to-back 33rd-place finishes during the Chase for the NASCAR NEXTEL Cup finally ended his chances.

Still, Dale Jr. finished in fifth place overall. That places him solidly among the favorites entering the 2005 season.

2004 Results

Races: 36
Points: 6,368
Overall finish: 5th
Victories: 6
Top-5 finishes: 16
Top-10 finishes: 21

FAST FACTS

♦ Dale Jr. has finished among the top 10 in the points standings three of the last four seasons.

♦ Dale is the son of legendary driver Dale Earnhardt Sr. and the grandson of Ralph Earnhardt, a member of the International Motorsports Hall of Fame.

66 *[Counting points] just wears you out. It's not much fun. What's fun is getting out there and giving your all—you know, just going at it. That's what we're going to do.* **99**

—Dale Earnhardt Jr., who didn't want to get caught up in "scoreboard watching" in 2004.

Jeff Gordon

Stats

Born: August 4, 1971
Birthplace: Vallejo, CA
NASCAR debut: 1992
Career victories: 69*

*as of the start of the 2005 season

Jeff Gordon hears it all the time: With four career NASCAR championships, can he match the all-time record of seven, shared by legendary drivers Richard Petty and Dale Earnhardt? Jeff's answer is the same all the time: Let me get to number five first.

No one else in NASCAR history stands between Gordon and the two record holders. But since winning his fourth championship in 2001, Jeff has had to settle for several near misses: fourth in 2002 and 2003, then third in 2004. Last season was the closest. Jeff needed a victory in the season-ending Ford 400 to take the title away from Kurt Busch. However, Jeff finished third in the race—and an agonizingly close 16 points away from that elusive fifth championship.

Still, the 2004 season was a resounding success. Jeff won five races, including one that has special meaning for him—the Brickyard 400 at the Indianapolis Motor Speedway. It was his fourth victory at the famous track, equaling the mark set by the open-wheel racers (A.J. Foyt, Al Unser, and Rick Mears) that Jeff idolized as a youngster in Indiana.

2004 Results

Races: 36
Points: 6,490
Overall finish: 3rd
Victories: 5
Top-5 finishes: 16
Top-10 finishes: 25

24

FAST FACTS

♦ Midway through the 2004 season, Jeff earned four consecutive poles—just one short of the modern NASCAR record.

♦ Jeff has posted 11 consecutive top-10 finishes in the overall points standings.

> ❝ *This team, man, they are just really on top of things right now. It's so much fun going to the racetrack when you know you've got a chance at winning—just pretty much every weekend you feel like you've got some kind of a shot at it.* ❞

—Jeff Gordon, during a midseason stretch in 2004
when he won three of six races and finished
in the top five each week.

Kevin Harvick

Stats

Born: December 8, 1975
Birthplace: Bakersfield, CA
NASCAR debut: 2001
Career victories: 4*

*as of the start of the 2005 season

They call Kevin Harvick "Happy" because, off the track, he's always got a smile on his face and a kind word for the media, racing fans, and his fellow drivers. But don't let that sunny disposition or the pleasant nickname fool you. On the track, Kevin is as fierce a competitor as there is in the NASCAR series.

As the driver who succeeded Dale Earnhardt Sr. on Richard Childress' racing team in 2001, Harvick inherited "The Intimidator's" hard-charging racing style. While he's never backed down from bumping fenders or "trading paint," Kevin also can finesse his way around the track. In short, he'll do whatever it takes to move to the front of the pack.

Harvick opened 2004 with a fourth-place finish at the Daytona 500, and he spent much of the first half of the season ranked among NASCAR's top 10 in the points standings. A midyear slump cost him a spot in the "Chase for the NASCAR NEXTEL Cup," but Kevin rebounded with a strong finish. He had five top-10 finishes in the last 10 races of 2004, fueling optimism for 2005.

2004 Results

Races: 36
Points: 4,228
Overall finish: 14th
Victories: 0
Top-5 finishes: 5
Top-10 finishes: 14

FAST FACTS

♦ In 2001, Kevin raced full time in both the NASCAR Cup Series and the series just below the NASCAR Cup Series—a grueling 69 races in all!

♦ Kevin's first NASCAR Cup Series win came in only the third start of his career. He edged Jeff Gordon to win the Cracker Barrel Old Country Store 500 in 2001.

" *Winning the Brickyard 400 is the biggest thing I've done in my career. Obviously, you can't win your first race twice.* **"**

—Kevin Harvick, who fulfilled a childhood dream by winning in 2003 at the famed Indianapolis Motor Speedway.

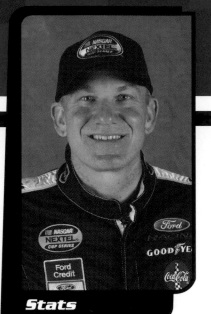

Dale Jarrett

Stats

Born: November 26, 1956
Birthplace: Hickory, NC
NASCAR debut: 1984
Career victories: 31*

*as of the start of the 2005 season

At age 48, Dale Jarrett could easily relax and count his career earnings, play golf, or ease his way into a NASCAR broadcast booth. But that's not for him. This wily, gray-haired veteran remains in dogged pursuit of his second NASCAR championship.

Don't count him out because of his age, either. It was only six seasons ago, in 1999, that Dale won his first points championship. At 42, he was the oldest driver ever to win the title for the first time.

Jarrett, a three-time winner of the famous Daytona 500, was a regular championship contender in the late 1990s and early 2000s. He strung together eight consecutive top-10 finishes in the points standings until falling to 26th in 2003. After such a disappointing season, Dale was not seen as a contender for the 2004 title. However, while he didn't win any races in 2004, Jarrett was one of NASCAR's most consistent drivers. He compiled 14 top-10 finishes, including six top-fives. He narrowly missed out on qualifying for the Chase for the NASCAR NEXTEL Cup, and finished the season in 15th place in the overall standings.

88

Races: 36
Points: 4,214
Overall finish: 15th
Victories: 0
Top-5 finishes: 6
Top-10 finishes: 14

FAST FACTS

♦ An outstanding all-around athlete, Dale was offered a golf scholarship by the University of South Carolina. The school also wanted him to play football.

♦ Dale is the son of Ned Jarrett, one of NASCAR's greatest champions in the 1960s.

66 *You dream about winning a race like that—racing door-to-door.* 99

—Dale Jarrett, reflecting on the first victory of his career, a win by a mere eight inches over Davey Allison at the 1991 Champion 400 in Michigan.

Jimmie Johnson

Stats

Born: September 17, 1975
Birthplace: El Cajon, CA
NASCAR debut: 2001
Career victories: 14*

*as of the start of the 2005 season

In Jimmie Johnson's three full seasons in the NASCAR Cup Series, he has finished fifth, second, and second in the overall standings. Is a points championship in his future? Most stock car fans will say one is perhaps as soon as this season.

Jimmie's strong finish to the 2004 season certainly bodes well for 2005. Six races from the end of the year, Johnson was struggling in eighth place. He was among the competitors in the Chase for the NASCAR NEXTEL Cup, but far behind leader Kurt Busch. His roller-coaster season to that point had included 16 top-10s, but also several points-killing DNFs ("did not finish").

Then, Jimmie put the pedal to the metal. He won the UAW-GM Quality 500 in mid-October. Then the Subway 500 the next week. And the Bass Pro Shops MBNA 500 the week after that. Suddenly, he was back in the points race. When Johnson won the Mountain Dew Southern 500 in the next-to-last event of the year, he had a real shot at the title.

Jimmie needed to win the final race, the Ford 500 in Homestead, Florida. He gave it a run but finished second—and second in the overall standings, just eight points behind Kurt Busch. It was the closest finish in NASCAR history.

2004 Results

Races: 36
Points: 6,498
Overall finish: 2nd
Victories: 8
Top-5 finishes: 20
Top-10 finishes: 23

48

FAST FACTS

♦ Jimmie won eight races in 2004, more than any other NASCAR driver.

♦ Jimmie drives the No. 48 car that is co-owned by fellow NASCAR star Jeff Gordon.

> 66 *I wish we could have gotten the job done, but we can leave here tonight knowing we gave 100 percent and gave everything that we could. We just came up short. We'll just come back [in 2005] and try harder.* 99

—Jimmie Johnson, after narrowly missing out on a
NASCAR points title in the last race of the 2004 season.

Kasey Kahne

Stats

Born: April 10, 1980
Birthplace: Enumclaw, WA
NASCAR debut: 2004
Career victories: 0*

*as of the start of the 2005 season

Kasey Kahne knew he had some big shoes to fill when he took over for veteran Bill Elliott as a full-time driver for Ray Evernham's racing team in 2004. For more than two decades, Elliott was one of the most popular and most successful drivers in NASCAR.

But with Kahne behind the wheel, the Evernham team hasn't missed a step. Kasey was far and away the top rookie in the NASCAR series in last season, when he finished 13th in the season standings. He was in the top 10 entering the last race before the cutoff for the Chase for the NASCAR NEXTEL Cup, but spun out midway through the Chevy Rock and Roll 400 in Richmond, Virginia. That forced him to lose too much ground, and he finished the race in 24th place, and outside the top 10 for the season.

Still, Kasey's marvelous rookie year was marked by four poles and five runner-up finishes, including back-to-back seconds in just the second and third official NASCAR Cup Series races of his young career. That helped Kahne, who turned 25 years old two months into the 2005 season, quickly build a considerable following for himself.

2004 Results

Races: 36
Points: 4,274
Overall finish: 13th
Victories: 0
Top-5 finishes: 13
Top-10 finishes: 14

FAST FACTS

♦ Kasey began his racing career on dirt tracks in his home state of Washington. He raced small open-wheel cars called Micro Midgets, and he won four races in his very first season.

♦ In his 2004 online diary, Kasey listed his goals at the beginning of his initial season: to win the Raybestos Rookie of the Year and to finish in the top 15 in points. Mission accomplished.

" *Meeting the fans and feeling their passion for our sport provides instant energy.* **"**

—Second-year driver Kasey Kahne, already a popular face in the NASCAR series, who feeds off the enthusiasm of race fans.

Matt Kenseth

Stats

Born: March 10, 1972
Birthplace: Cambridge, WI
NASCAR debut: 1998
Career victories: 9*

*as of the start of the 2005 season

Matt Kenseth enters the 2005 season hoping to reclaim the points championship that he won in 2003, his fourth full season in the NASCAR Cup Series. He followed that with a solid eighth-place finish in 2004.

If Matt can make it back to the top, he'll do it in his usual understated way. Don't expect to find Matt starring in any MTV shows or pitching a lot of different products in national advertisements. He's not NASCAR's biggest or flashiest star, but he is one of its most consistent drivers.

That steady, but not spectacular, manner is the way Matt won his points title in 2003. He finished among the top 10 in 25 of the 36 races that season, though he won only one race.

After a ninth-place finish in the season-opening Daytona 500, he won his first race in almost a year by taking the checkered flag at the Subway 400. The next time out, he won again at the UAW-DaimlerChrysler 400. It was a resounding answer to critics who said that Matt raced only to gain points, and not to win.

2004 Results

Races: 36
Points: 6,069
Overall finish: 8th
Victories: 2
Top-5 finishes: 8
Top-10 finishes: 16

FAST FACTS

♦ Matt won five races in 2002 the most on the NASCAR Cup Series circuit that year.

♦ Matt's first full season racing in the NASCAR Cup Series was in 2000; he was named Raybestos Rookie of the Year after finishing 14th in the points standings.

People have said that we can't lead laps and we can't win races, that we just go out to finish seventh every week. So it was awesome to go out and do it. To come out of the box and win right away is great.

—Matt Kenseth, after taking the checkered flag at the Subway 400 in just the second race of the 2004 season.

Bobby Labonte

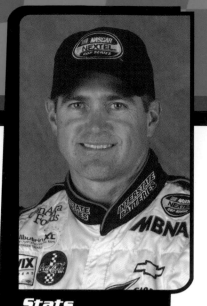

Stats

Born: May 8, 1964
Birthplace: Corpus Christi, TX
NASCAR debut: 1991
Career victories: 21*

*as of the start of the 2005 season

Bobby Labonte enters the 2005 season trying to recapture the magic that carried him to the NASCAR championship in 2000. He won four times in 34 starts that year to ascend to the top of the racing world, but fell to as low as 20th place in 2003.

It looked like Bobby might be back on the championship road last season, when he stood sixth in the overall standings midway through the year. But after a change of crew chiefs in July, Bobby's team struggled. The No.18 car finished outside the top 10 in each of the next 15 races, slipping in the standings and out of contention for the season championship.

Though it was too late to make much of an impact on the final standings, Bobby posted consecutive ninth-place finishes in November, a positive step he hopes to carry over into 2005.

Bobby's brother, Terry, is still going to run a limited schedule in 2005, so Terry and Bobby will still race against each other. One of Bobby's greatest days in NASCAR came in 1996, when he won the Napa 500 in Atlanta. That same day, Terry finished fifth to wrap up his second NASCAR points title. Bobby, Terry, and their mom and dad all gathered together in Victory Lane.

2004 Results

Races: 36
Points: 4,277
Overall finish: 12th
Victories: 0
Top-5 finishes: 5
Top-10 finishes: 11

18

FAST FACTS

♦ Six of his Bobby's 21 career victories have come at the Atlanta Motor Speedway.
♦ Bobby and Terry Labonte form the only brother combination each to win a NASCAR Cup Series points title.

> **66** *It's always cool to win the last race because you can celebrate the off season just a little longer than the next guy.* **99**
>
> —Bobby Labonte, who's had a knack for closing the NASCAR season with a victory—he's done it four times since 1996.

Mark Martin

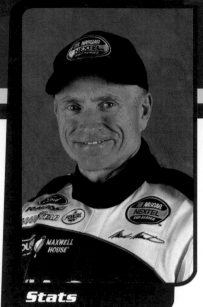

Stats

Born: January 9, 1959
Birthplace: Batesville, AR
NASCAR debut: 1981
Career victories: 34*

*as of the start of the 2005 season

Mark Martin hopes things get off to a faster start in 2005 than he did in 2004. He was determined to improve on his 17th-place finish in the points standings in 2003. However, he got off to a shaky start, finishing last in the Daytona 500. He managed only seven laps before his engine gave out, and thus began the season in 43rd place.

Luckily for Martin, it was not a sign of things to come. In fact, with no place to go but up, the No. 6 car did just that. Martin had several top-10 finishes before notching the 34th victory of his illustrious career at the MBNA 400 in June. By September, he had qualified for the Chase for the NASCAR NEXTEL Cup.

Though Martin's pursuit of his first points championship fell just 107 points short, the 2004 season turned out to be one of the most rewarding of his career. At the end, however, he was exhausted from the demands of chasing a championship, so the 46-year-old driver announced that 2005 would be his last season as a full-time NASCAR driver.

2004 Results

Races: 36
Points: 6,399
Overall finish: 4th
Victories: 1
Top-5 finishes: 10
Top-10 finishes: 15

FAST FACTS

♦ Mark finished in the top 10 in the NASCAR points standings each season from 1989 through 2000.

♦ Mark's 34 career victories (entering 2005) rank 10th among all drivers in NASCAR's modern era (1972 to the present).

> **66** *Chasing for the Cup in 2004 has definitely been the most consuming season of my life. No one can understand how important it has been for me to be a contender.* **99**

—Mark Martin, one of the greatest drivers in NASCAR history, just before he announced his retirement.

Jeremy Mayfield

Stats

Born: May 27, 1969
Birthplace: Owensboro, KY
NASCAR debut: 1994
Career victories: 4*

*as of the start of the 2005 season

Jeremy Mayfield showed a flair for the dramatic in 2004. Winless in his last 143 races, he was in 14th place as the Chase for the NASCAR NEXTEL Cup approached. Only the top ten drivers would qualify for the Chase. He did exactly what he needed to do at the Chevy Rock and Roll 400—take the checkered flag. Mayfield's victory lifted him to ninth place in the standings and earned him a spot in the top 10.

Unfortunately, Jeremy's dreams of his first points championship suffered a severe blow just one week later, when he was among the drivers caught up in an on-track fender-bender between fellow drivers Robby Gordon and Greg Biffle. The resulting crash took out Mayfield, who could not finish the race. He had several more DNFs ("did not finish") in the season's remaining races, and finished 10th in the overall standings.

Still, it was the best season for Jeremy since his career-best seventh place finish in 1998. That year, it appeared that he would be one of the drivers to watch in the coming seasons. Though he didn't seriously contend for the title again until last year, good things seem to be on the horizon for him again.

2004 Results

Races: 36
Points: 6,000
Overall finish: 10th
Victories: 1
Top-5 finishes: 5
Top-10 finishes: 13

FAST FACTS

♦ Jeremy's first career victory came in 1998 at the Pocono 500 in Pennsylvania.

♦ Jeremy was born in the same hometown (Owensboro, Kentucky) as fellow NASCAR veteran Michael Waltrip

66 *The new places are just unbelievable, and by the time you think that's the most excited you've seen a bunch of race fans, the next week you go back to a place you've seen forever, and they're the same way! It doesn't ever seem that there's a dull moment in this world.* **99**

—Jeremy Mayfield, on the enthusiasm he finds from stock car fans on each stop of the NASCAR schedule.

Jamie McMurray

Stats

Born: June 3, 1976
Birthplace: Joplin, MO
NASCAR debut: 2002
Career victories: 1*

*as of the start of the 2005 season

February marks a fresh start for every driver in the NASCAR NEXTEL Cup Series. But Jamie McMurray goes into the 2005 season with perhaps more incentive than most after coming oh-so-close to participating in the first Chase for the NASCAR NEXTEL Cup in 2004.

When the final 10 qualifiers were set to compete after 26 races of the season, Jamie stood on the outside looking in—in 11th place. He had a chance to crack the top 10 in the final race before the cutoff, the Chevy Rock and Roll 400, but a ninth-place finish in that race left him just 15 points short.

Still, the 2004 season wasn't a total loss for the up-and-coming McMurray. He won three races in the series just below the NASCAR NEXTEL Cup, including back-to-back checkered flags in November, and a NASCAR Craftsman Truck Series race, too. Combined with the NASCAR Cup Series race he won in Concord, North Carolina, in 2002, McMurray became only the eighth driver in NASCAR history to win at all three levels.

Jamie also earned a cool $1 million bonus for finishing 11th in the points standings in 2004—a pretty nice consolation prize for missing the Chase!

2004 Results

Races: 36
Points: 4,597
Overall finish: 11th
Victories: 0
Top-5 finishes: 9
Top-10 finishes: 23

FAST FACTS

♦ In 2002, Jamie became the first driver in NASCAR's modern era to win in just the second race of his career.

♦ Jamie's first full season on the NASCAR circuit was in 2003, when he earned Raybestos Rookie of the Year honors for placing 13th in the overall standings.

66 *It's probably the most disappointing thing that's happened to me in my racing career, to come that close.* 99

—Jamie McMurray, on standing 11th at the cutoff point for 2004's Chase for the NASCAR NEXTEL Cup, which was open to the top 10 drivers heading into the last 10 races.

Joe Nemechek

Stats

Born: September 26, 1963
Birthplace: Lakeland, FL
NASCAR debut: 1993
Career victories: 4*

*as of the start of the 2005 season

Whatever Joe Nemechek does on the racetrack in 2005, it'll be tough to top his performance at the Kansas Speedway last October. That's when he had the racing weekend of his life.

First, on Friday, Joe ran the fastest qualifying lap for the Banquet 400 to earn the pole position (the best starting position—the inside spot on the front row) for that Sunday's NASCAR NEXTEL Cup Series race. It was the second consecutive pole for the man who earned the nickname "Front Row Joe" for a string of poles earned in earlier seasons.

Then, driving on Saturday in the series just below the NASCAR NEXTEL Cup, Nemechek took the checkered flag when he edged Greg Biffle by just half a car length in the Mr. Goodcents 300. Finally, on Sunday, Joe completed a rare triple play when he won the Banquet 400. He did it in dramatic fashion, too, racing door-to-door and bumping with veteran Ricky Rudd before winning by about a car length.

It was the fourth NASCAR Cup Series win of Nemechek's career, after which "Front Row Joe" admitted he liked the sound of "Victory Lane Joe" even better.

2004 Results

Races: 36
Points: 3,878
Overall finish: 19th
Victories: 1
Top-5 finishes: 3
Top-10 finishes: 9

FAST FACTS

◆ Upon winning last season's Banquet 400, Joe paid tribute to the men and women of the armed forces; his car is sponsored by the U.S. Army.

◆ Though Joe has not finished higher than 15th in the NASCAR Cup Series standings, he is a former champion in the series just below the NASCAR NEXTEL Cup Series.

66 *We're not the big powerhouse out there, but we have quality people who are there to get the job done. It's neat when you outrun the big three or the big four, you know?* **99**

—Joe Nemechek, on competing against some of the bigger-name stars in the NASCAR series.

Ryan Newman

Stats

Born: December 8, 1977
Birthplace: South Bend, IN
NASCAR debut: 2000
Career victories: 11*

*as of the start of the 2005 season

For Ryan Newman, there's only one way to drive a race car—fast! Ryan's first full season in the NASCAR Cup Series was in 2002, and he earned the pole position as the fastest qualifier six times. That was more than any other driver that year and the most ever by a rookie. In 2003, he earned 11 poles, again the most on the circuit. In 2004, it was nine poles, marking the third consecutive year that he won NASCAR's pole award.

Not only does Ryan usually have the fastest car at the beginning of a race, but also he often has the fastest car at the end of the race. He won eight events in 2003, more than any other driver that season, and he enters 2005 with 11 career victories. Unfortunately, Ryan's pedal-to-the-metal racing often translates to all-or-nothing finishes. He's had 21 DNFs ("did not finish") since 2002, including nine last year.

In 2004, as expected, he qualified for the Chase for the NASCAR NEXTEL Cup, and he finished in seventh place. The 10 races in 2004 proved to be a mirror of Ryan's career. He had a first (at the MBNA America 400), a second, and a third, but he also had finishes of 30th, 33rd (twice), and 34th place. That seems typical for Ryan—his hard-charging racing style usually either puts him out in front of the pack or out of contention.

2004 Results

Races: 36
Points: 6,180
Overall finish: 7th
Victories: 2
Top-5 finishes: 11
Top-10 finishes: 14

FAST FACTS

♦ Ryan's seventh-place finish in 2004 was his third top 10 in as many full-time seasons in the NASCAR Cup Series.

♦ Ryan has a degree in vehicle structure engineering from Purdue University.

> **" I always say that I don't believe in luck and superstition and all that stuff. But if there Is such a thing as bad luck, it trailed our team all last season. "**

—Ryan Newman, after his 2004 season ended with a cut tire in the final race just three laps from an apparent victory.

Elliott Sadler

Stats

Born: April 30, 1975
Birthplace: Emporia, VA
NASCAR debut: 1998
Career victories: 3*

*as of the start of the 2005 season

Elliott Sadler made some big moves on the racetrack in 2004. He secured a spot in the Chase for the NASCAR NEXTEL Cup by winning the Pop Secret 500 at California's Fontana Speedway. He did that by passing Mark Martin and Brian Vickers with a daring move late in the race. Earlier Elliott won the Samsung/Radio Shack 500 in Fort Worth, Texas. In that race, he held off rookie Kasey Kahne to win by just two one-hundredths of a second.

However, the biggest move Elliott made was in the overall points standings. After finishing in 23rd place in 2003, he leaped 14 spots to number nine in 2004. Nobody else in the NASCAR Cup Series made as big a jump up last season. That makes Sadler one of the drivers to watch in 2005.

Actually, Elliott has been considered a young driver to watch since graduating to a full-time ride in the NASCAR Cup Series in 1999. He had been one of the top drivers in the series just below the NASCAR NEXTEL Cup in 1997 and 1998. However, after several disappointing seasons with a couple of different racing teams, Elliott shifted to the Robert Yates team in 2003. That turned out to be another of Elliott's good moves.

2004 Results

Races: 36
Points: 6,024
Overall finish: 9th
Victories: 2
Top-5 finishes: 8
Top-10 finishes: 14

FAST FACTS

♦ Before 2004, Elliott's lone career win had come at 2001's Ford City 500 in Bristol, Tennessee.

♦ Elliott's older brother, Hermie, is a fellow NASCAR driver who once was the Raybestos Rookie of the Year in the series just below the NASCAR NEXTEL Cup.

66 *I made the best move I've probably ever made as a race car driver. I got on the outside, got a lot of grip, and went to the lead. I was like, 'Wow, this is cool!'* 99

—Elliott Sadler, on winning the Pop Secret 500 in 2004 by passing the leaders after the final pit stop.

Tony Stewart

Stats

Born: May 20, 1971
Birthplace: Columbus, IN
NASCAR debut: 1999
Career victories: 19*

*as of the start of the 2005 season

If past performances are any indication of future results, you can expect to see Tony Stewart's name among the contenders for the NASCAR championship in 2005. That's because in his first six seasons in the NASCAR Cup Series, Tony has finished fourth, sixth, second, first, seventh, and sixth in the overall standings.

Then again, Stewart has been successful whenever he's gotten behind the wheel of any race car. Tony grew up in Indiana, less than an hour's drive from the Indianapolis Motor Speedway. He dreamed of becoming a famous open-wheel driver, and his dream came true when he won the Indy Racing League championship in 1997. Two years later he turned his attention to NASCAR full time, and soon became a stock car champion as well.

Though Tony is known as one of the fiercest NASCAR competitors, he is one of its most caring drivers, too. In 2003, he started the Tony Stewart Foundation to support various charitable causes. In 2004, he and fellow driver Kyle Petty shared USA Weekend's award for the Most Caring Athlete for starting a fantasy camp for sick kids.

20

Races: 36

Points: 6,326

Overall finish: 6th

Victories: 2

Top-5 finishes: 10

Top-10 finishes: 19

FAST FACTS

♦ Tony won NASCAR's points title in 2002. He took the checkered flag in three races that year and held off Mark Martin by 38 points in the overall standings.

♦ Tony bought a racetrack last year. He purchased the Eldora Speedway in Rossburg, Ohio, a half-mile clay oval on which he competed many times earlier in his career.

" *He never pressured me to be the best race car driver in the world, but he did pressure me to be the best race car driver that I could be.* "

—Tony Stewart, on a lifelong lesson that he learned from his dad.

Rusty Wallace

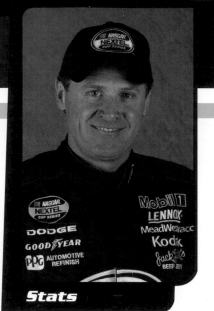

Stats

Born: August 14, 1956

Birthplace: St. Louis, MO

NASCAR debut: 1980

Career victories: 55*

*as of the start of the 2005 season

One of the hardest decisions any great athlete has to face is knowing when to retire. For Rusty Wallace, the end of the 2005 season will be that time. He's announced that the 2005 season will be his last as a full-time driver in NASCAR.

Rusty will retire with a legacy as one of the top drivers in NASCAR history. Since his first full season in 1984, he's never finished lower than 19th in the overall standings. He won at least one race each year from 1986 through 2001, and his 55 career victories equal the sixth-best mark of the modern era. He is a two-time driver of the year (1988 and 1993) and a NASCAR champion (1989). In fact, just about the only thing missing from his stellar career is a win in the Daytona 500—something he hopes to change in 2005.

Rusty describes himself as the youngest-feeling 48-year-old around, and his hectic "retirement" plans prove it. He intends to work on the team he owns in the series just below the NASCAR NEXTEL Cup and on the Penske racing team, of which he is part-owner. He also plans to take a more active role in his car dealership and in his son Steve's racing career.

2004 Results

Races: 36
Points: 3,960
Overall finish: 16th
Victories: 1
Top-5 finishes: 3
Top-10 finishes: 11

FAST FACTS

♦ Rusty finished among the top 10 in the points standings all but one year from 1986 through 2002.

♦ Rusty won a remarkable 18 races over the course of the 1993 and 1994 seasons. His lone points title, though, came in 1989, when he took the checkered flag six times.

❝ *It's time—I feel it. I know I'm doing the right thing, and I feel good about it.* **❞**

—Veteran driver Rusty Wallace, who has decided to retire from full-time racing after the 2005 season.

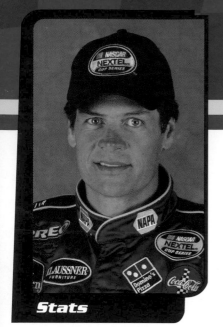

Michael Waltrip

Stats

Born: April 30, 1963
Birthplace: Owensboro, KY
NASCAR debut: 1985
Career victories: 4*

*as of the start of the 2005 season

With just four victories in more than 600 career starts entering the 2005 season, Michael Waltrip may not be the most winning driver in NASCAR, but he is one of its most visible. That's because each of Michael's wins has come in high-profile races on the storied tracks of Daytona and Talladega.

Those tracks are the superspeedways where the cars race at top speeds and in packs of three or four cars bunched three and four wide on the straightaways. Waltrip calls it "over-the-top entertainment" for the fans, and such events attract even non-racing fans to tune in on television. Michael has excelled in those exciting events, winning the Daytona 500 two times, the Pepsi 400 at Daytona, and the EA Sports 500 at Talladega.

Only eight drivers have won the Daytona 500—the "Super Bowl of NASCAR"—more than once. Michael's first victory in the famous race came in 2001. The next came two years later to open the 2003 season.

2004 Results

Races: 36
Points: 3,878
Overall finish: 20th
Victories: 0
Top-5 finishes: 2
Top-10 finishes: 9

FAST FACTS

♦ Michael started 463 races in his career before finally notching his first victory at the Daytona 500 in 2001.

♦ Michael is the younger brother of Darrell Waltrip, a three-time NASCAR champion in the 1980s.

> 66 *I think we're building a good foundation, and we can enter 2005 in better shape than we've ever been. I feel like we will show results right away.* 99

—Michael Waltrip, on getting a head start for this season
by working with his new crew chief in the final
races of 2004.

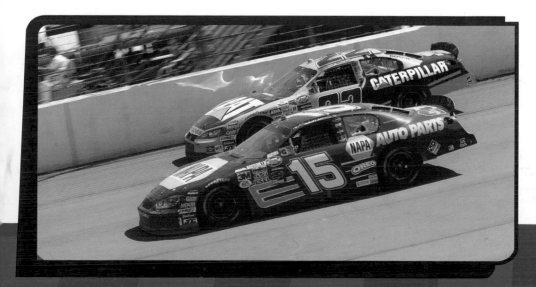

MORE NASCAR RACING!

There's a lot more to NASCAR than just the NASCAR NEXTEL Cup Series. Two other NASCAR series feature great racing thrills, top stars, and fun for racing fans.

The series just below the NASCAR NEXTEL Cup Series takes place on many of the same tracks in the top series. The cars are slightly longer and wider than NASCAR NEXTEL Cup Series cars, so speeds are slightly slower. The races run for shorter distances, too. However, that doesn't stop top drivers from putting the pedal to the metal in exciting races. In 2005, this series has 35 races on its schedule, from February to October.

Martin Truex, Jr., is the defending champion. Kyle Busch, Kurt Busch's younger brother, finished second. Trying to knock Martin and Kyle out of the top spots will be dozens of great drivers. Some of them will be familiar to fans from NASCAR NEXTEL Cup Series races. In 2004, NASCAR NEXTEL Series drivers Michael Waltrip, Dale Earnhardt Jr., Jamie McMurray, and Kevin Harvick all won races in the series just below the NASCAR NEXTEL Cup Series. Dale Earnhardt Jr. is among the stars who own cars in this series, too.

Cars aren't the only vehicles racing in NASCAR. The NASCAR Craftsman Truck Series, which celebrates its 10th anniversary in 2005, features top drivers in specially modified pickup trucks. These aren't your family trucks, however. They can reach speeds up to 160 miles per hour! In 2005, Bobby Hamilton will try to defend his 2004 title in the series' 25 races.